ATLANTIS

JOURNEY FROM THE INNER TEMPLE

APRIL AUTRY

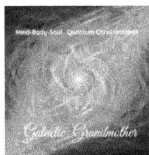

ALSO BY APRIL AUTRY

Galactic Grandmother Past Life Series

MY LIFE WITH JESUS

ESCAPE FROM MALDEK

Galactic Grandmother Spiritual Journey Series

WORKING IN THE QUANTUM FIELD, BOOK 1 & 2

MULTIDIMENSIONAL ASPECTS - HIGHER SELVES

PROLOGUE

In 2014, I sat in a chair with my feet soaking in warm water, and watched a woman prepare the machine for my ionic foot detox. I had not experienced this before, and was quite interested to see how it worked. The woman was very pleasant, and explained that following the detox, she would give me a foot massage. Needless to say, I was in a happy, relaxed mood and allowed any tension in my body to drift away.

I was still looking at this woman, when suddenly a vivid scene flashed into my mind's eye. I saw this woman, this stranger that sat in front of me, in a temple. I knew the woman in the temple was my daughter, and I was saying goodbye to her. I was leaving and knew I would not return. This was all I saw, yet the emotions stayed with me.

My happy, relaxed state dissolved, and had been replaced with grief and sadness. I wanted to shout out "I know you!" to the woman near my feet, yet managed to discreetly say, "You look familiar."

She also felt I looked familiar, and as we explored how we might know each other, it turned out the woman doing my foot detox was a Reiki healer, and psychic counselor.

With her spiritual beliefs in mind, I told her about my vision, and that I believed her to be my daughter in a previous incarnation. At that time, I knew the temple was ancient, yet I wasn't able to place a location on it.

We have since become dear friends, and understand that we are soul family. We have incarnated again in this lifetime to play roles for each other, and assist each other's growth.

ATLANTIS, JOURNEY FROM THE INNER TEMPLE is the past life that began with meeting my friend, and subsequently was revealed when I tapped into my akashic record of that life.

CHAPTER 1

I stood within the marble temple. The floor, high walls, and round columns were pristine white and once offered me comfort, yet now my heart ached with love and pain. I stood watching my beloved daughter pace. She walked back and forth at the rear of the inner temple and the silhouette of her long, black gown contrasted sharply with the white marble. I admired her red hair which fell down her back, and I memorized every exquisite detail of her.

I waited not wanting to ask, yet compelled as a mother, needing to know that there was nothing more I could do. She had told me her decision. I knew that I could not persuade her, nor alter her course. My chest was tight, so tight it was hard to breath. Tears spilled down my face.

"Are you sure?"

She stopped and turned to look at me. I gasped. How could I leave her? My child, my heart.

"You must go." She said firmly, "You must go now."

I wanted to hold her just once more, to try and change her mind, yet I sank into the knowing of our destiny. I nodded. My throat had tightened so much, that I had to will my body to speak those final words.

"I love you."

"I love you." She said, then turned away and began her pacing again.

I knew her scientific mind was working, thinking of what else she might do to prevent the inevitable, so I looked once more at my beloved before spinning on my heel to leave.

~

I HAD ENJOYED my life on Atlantis. I was the daughter of a wealthy merchant, that followed my spiritual inclinations into the temple at an early age. I blossomed in the environment of spiritual pursuit, loving the peace and the companionship of other girls that shared my interests. As my knowledge and experience grew, my devotion to the Great Mother was rewarded by initiation as a temple priestess. Following this, I had access to the secret schools of ancient wisdom, and I savored learning what was given at each stage of my development. I had no plan other than to devote my life to the Great Mother and the temple, yet life had another plan for me.

~

EACH YEAR A FEAST is held at the temple, to honor the men in the warrior ranks that protect us. The High Priestess performs ceremonies for their safety and good health. All the priestesses are involved with the feast by serving food, pouring wine, and singing songs. Men are allowed on the temple grounds, and inside the temple for ceremonies, yet a room full of young virile men was quite a sight for the priestesses. We were warned not to have conversations with them, that we were to treat them respectfully as honored guests, and nothing more. Yet, as the dinner progressed and more wine was poured, the warriors tried harder to get our attention. They whispered how pretty we were, and when a young priestess blushed, the men laughed. I became annoyed and when a warrior reached out to grab my gown, I turned quickly to slap his hand away.

Suddenly the man that grabbed my gown was picked up from behind. I saw hands slip under his arms and he was lifted up and carried out of the gathering room by a very tall muscular warrior. Everyone in the hall became quiet and watched until the door closed behind them. The others went back to talking, yet I stood waiting to see who might return.

The door opened and the tall warrior that carried the other out, walked back into the gathering room. Again, the room became quiet as we watched this warrior walk toward me. I did not move, and soon the warrior stood before me. I looked up at his face and felt myself take a deep breath. I looked into his blue eyes and thought he was the most beautiful man I had ever seen. He had red hair that curled softly around his head, and then he smiled. He was looking back at me, I felt embarrassed and looked down.

"I am sorry," he said.

I looked back up at him.

"He should not have touched you and will be punished." He told me.

I nodded.

"Thank you," I said, "He didn't hurt me," I stammered, "I hope his punishment will not be severe."

"He will be punished for going against orders," he told me.

I listened and waited for him to say more, when the High Priestess walked to us and put her hand on my shoulder.

"Did he hurt you?" She asked.

"No, I just told him I was not hurt." I said.

The High Priestess looked at the tall warrior. "Thank you."

The tall warrior bowed to the High Priestess, then straightened up.

"His punishment will be to work at the temple, doing whatever you need him to do."

The High Priestess smiled. "I have work he can do."

It was agreed that the tall warrior would bring him back and supervise him while he was on temple grounds.

"Blessings son." The High Priestess told him.

She took my arm to leave and I looked back at him, happy that I would see him again.

The next day the High Priestess asked me to serve them food and water, and to speak with the tall warrior while he supervised the other warrior's work. So it was that we saw each other many times, spoke of our families and of our lives, until that day we looked into each other's eyes, and felt the love that began and has never ended.

~

It was not unusual for a young woman in temple training to fall in love and leave, but I did not want to leave my temple life, and my lover was a dedicated warrior rising in the ranks. We met many times out of sight from others, lying in the garden at night, and after several big moons had passed, I was with child. I knew that I must meet with the High Priestess, so that I could make a special request, a request that had never been asked before. I feared that she would send me back to my family, so I avoided seeing her until my circumstances forced me.

I walked into the High Priestess's room and sat in a chair as she requested. She sat across from me and smiled.

"Why have you come?" She asked.

I felt ashamed, looked down and held my hands tightly in my lap.

"Do you need to tell me something?" She asked sweetly.

I looked up and saw a slight smile on her face. Suddenly I realized that she already knew what I would say.

"I am with child." I told her.

She nodded.

"I do not want to leave the temple." I said.

"Oh?" She asked.

"I am requesting to continue being a priestess, live at the temple, and raise my child here."

She nodded while she was thinking about my request.

"Your request is approved," she told me, "only you must live with your child separate from the other priestesses."

My eyes widened, and I was happy.

"You may build a house within the temple grounds."

"Thank you!" I was relieved yet curious. "Did you know already?"

The High Priestess looked out the window for a few moments, and when she turned back to me, she had a strange look on her face.

"During my prayers, I received information about our temple." She told me.

I sat up straight, she was sharing information with me! I never expected this.

"I was shown a warrior that would save our temple," she said, "he would save our temple because he loved a priestess that lived here."

My eyes widened.

"Save our temple?" I asked.

She nodded. "Our temple is what we teach."

I was confused.

"This temple was not always the beautiful structure it is today. It was simply a gathering place to teach and to honor the Great Mother." She told me.

"Oh." I said.

"The Gods told me a child would be born at the temple. The child of a priestess and a warrior." She said and smiled.

"Did you know it was me?" I asked.

"No, not until I saw you with him." She answered, "That is why I asked you to speak with him."

～

MY FATHER BUILT a beautiful house far behind the temple gardens, yet still within the temple walls, and provided servants that would live with me to care for the house and my child. The house was ready by the time my daughter was born, and her birth was celebrated by all at the temple. I loved my daughter, my new home, and the opportunity to continue my spiritual studies and duties. We even saw her father, when he returned to Atlantis after long periods of travel.

~

My DAUGHTER WAS a curious child that began exploring the garden as soon as she could walk. She loved playing outdoors, splashing her little hands in the water of the fountain, and chasing butterflies. We had cats that followed her indoors and outside, and my daughter gave them names, spoke to them, and the cats seemed to understand. She learned the words to songs that we sang in the temple, and was learning to read books, when my father came to visit. He watched her take apart her doll, then easily put it back together.

"Come here and show me your doll." He told her.

She brought her doll and he lifted her up on his lap.

"What is that?" He pointed to the doll's arm.

She tilted her head and looked at him with a puzzled expression. "That is her arm."

"Oh," he said, "what is that?"

He pointed to the doll's chest.

My daughter quickly said, "That is her chest, and inside is her heart."

My father looked up at me. "She needs a teacher!"

I knew he was right.

"She needs to learn more than what is taught here." He told me, "I will find a teacher for her."

My father found a teacher that came to our house, and my daughter blossomed. She was a dedicated student that was not swayed by the games that other children played at her age. She loved to read, and her teacher brought many books that she took outside to read. I saw her reading books daily, while sitting on a cushion in the shade of the trees, with her beloved cats lying beside her.

However, it was when the teacher brought ingredients for elixirs that my daughter really became excited. She found making elixirs for people and animals really got her excited. The teacher came to me one day with a smile on his face.

"We have a young scientist." He told me.

CHAPTER 2

⁂

My High Priestess had a wonderful life. She had started her temple training young like me, and lived her life as an example of the Great Mother. She loved the people and they loved her. She was known for her friendliness, her smile, and how she reached out to put her hand on shoulders when she spoke, or how she wrapped her arms around people before saying goodbye. She performed her duties even after she was old and frail, when devotees attended her and walked with her. I was one of those devotees for many years and became her confidant.

⁂

THE HIGH PRIESTESS and I walked from the temple after having performed a new moon ceremony. I held her arm as we descended the steps, then she stopped and looked up at the night sky.

"I will invite all the temples to join us for the next big moon. We will have a gathering." She told me.

"I will send messengers." I answered.

"I will make an important announcement." She said.

I looked at her and waited for her to tell me what the announcement would be, yet she began walking again and sang a song that she enjoyed.

Gatherings were three days of feasts and fun. We saw friends from the other temples, new priestesses would be initiated, and others received promotions and new assignments. High Priestesses from the other temples led us in spiritual activities, and I always learned something new. My daughter was twelve years old at this time, and we watched the moon each evening with anticipation.

"Look!" She said and pointed up.

The moon was almost fully round.

"Our guests will begin arriving soon." I told her.

~

THE SUN AROSE and our temple came to life. Morning devotions to the Great Mother were finished, we ate and many scurried around the temple grounds cleaning and preparing for visitors. Beds were prepared, flowers were cut from the gardens, and the kitchen had extra help with food for the festivities. When my daughter's teacher arrived at our home, I left to attend the High Priestess.

Another priestess helped me bath her in water scented with oils, and we dressed her in a gown the color of a ripe melon, before braiding flowers into her long white hair. She was happy and sang songs while we gathered items that she would need that day. We placed incense, candles, crystals, scrolls wrapped in fabric, gold necklaces with sacred symbols for the new priestesses, and gifts for the other temple High Priestesses in a small wooden wagon that we would pull to the temple gathering room.

The High Priestess looked around and was pleased.

"We are ready." She said and motioned for me to come.

I stepped to her and she took my arm. We walked from her rooms followed by the other priestess pulling the wagon, down the hall of the temple, stopping to look into the kitchen where she checked on the food. Then we passed a large room with tables and chairs, where the food would be served, and we saw flowers on each table along with candles that would be lit.

I felt the hand on my arm shaking and turned to look at the High Priestess. She smiled, yet she had tears in her eyes.

"I am fine." She said and patted my arm.

We came to the main gathering room of the temple and the High Priestess told us to put the wagon in a closet behind the alter. After doing this, we continued walking through the temple until we reached the public entrance and stopped. Flowers had been placed in large containers in every corner of the room, and on a table in the center of the room. The warm air enhanced their fragrance, and a slight breeze spread their welcoming smell out the large doors and into the courtyard.

The High Priestess nodded her head.

"I will receive our guests out here." She said and walked outside.

The large stone porch was covered and shady, with many couches, chairs and tables. The High Priestess picked a chair with a high back and soft cushions near the steps that entered the porch. She sat and looked at me.

"I need water, and then you may leave." She told me.

I was surprised because I expected to stay with her as she greeted guests, so I hesitated before leaving to get her water. The High Priestess looked at me.

"I am thirsty." She told me.

I left immediately and when I returned, I saw the other priestess leaning down, while the High Priestess whispered in her ear. As I approached, the priestess straightened up and took the water from me.

"Thank you." She said.

I stood there as she sat the water down on the table by the High Priestess.

"I won't be needing you until evening meal." The High Priestess told me.

I was perplexed as this had never happened before, yet I left before being told again.

~

I WANDERED through the temple and helped where I was needed. I checked the alter in the main gathering room, and brought wine, water and glasses there. I kept myself busy yet could not stop wondering if I had done something wrong or offended the High Priestess in any way. Instead of enjoying myself, I was worried and unable to relax. I decided to go home and be with my daughter.

I found her looking at a map as her teacher pointed to it. They looked up at me.

"You may stop early today." I told them. "This is a day of celebration!"

I smiled and tried to sound happy. My daughter and her teacher put away the books, and we said our goodbyes.

I took my daughter for a walk around the temple grounds. We saw many people that we knew and stopped to talk. We went into the kitchen and made plates of food which we ate outside, sitting by a fountain. My daughter was excited, happy and talked without stopping. I laughed with her at many of her observations, and our enjoyment of the day was only surpassed by our love for each other.

"I will sit by the High Priestess for the official dinner." I told her.

She looked at me puzzled. "You always do! Why are you telling me this?"

I laughed, "I wanted you to know that while I sit with the High Priestess, I will think of you."

She smiled, then began speaking of how her friend had found a frog in the fountain where we sat. I watched her and listened, yet at the same time I realized that she had grown up in the temple. She knew temple protocols better than some of the new priestesses, so she never considered that I would sit anywhere else except by the High Priestess.

~

WE WERE BATHED and dressed in our finest gowns. I wore priestess jewelry as well as jewelry gifted to me from my family. I checked my daughter's hair, which had been braided and pinned on top of her head.

"I want to give you this." I said and handed her a small box that was on a table.

Her eyes lit up and she opened it.

"Oh! It's beautiful!" She cried out.

She held up the delicate gold necklace with a sparkling blue jewel that hung from it.

"My mother gave me that necklace when I was your age," I told her, "now I give it to you."

"Thank you!" She said and wrapped her arms around me.

"Let me put it on you." I told her, then slipped it around her neck, and locked the clasp.

I stood back and admired my daughter. "You are beautiful."

She reached up to hold the jewel on her necklace and smiled.

"You are too." She said sweetly.

I took her hand and we walked from our home toward the temple. It was an evening like many others on Atlantis, the sky was clear, the air was warm, and the fragrance of flowers made me want to breath in deeply. I felt immense gratitude for the opportunity to live in such a place, and to share its beauty with my daughter. Together we took the steps up to the temple entrance, and walked directly into the large dining hall, where we separated and took our seats.

⁓

THE DINNER WAS DELICIOUS, the conversations were punctuated with laughter, and when we were finished, I helped the High Priestess stand.

"Let us go into the gathering room." The High Priestess announced.

Everyone stood and waited for us to walk out first, then we led the way into the gathering room. We went to a long table set up in front of the alter and the High Priestess sat at the center of the table, with me and the other attending priestess on each side of her. The visiting High Priestesses and their attendants sat on both sides of us. We waited for the gathering room to fill with priestesses, and when all were seated, I helped my High Priestess stand so that she might speak.

"We invoke the Great Mother and all High Priestesses that have gone before to join us now."

After she said this, everyone in the room also said it.

"We allow the Great Mother's love to flow through us for all."

Again, the others repeated what she said.

"We begin sacred ceremonies in honor of the Great Mother."

Now all the High Priestesses stood and walked before the table, they called forth and initiated their new priestesses. Following this, the new priestesses received a piece of jewelry from each High Priestess, which signified they were welcome in all the temples. The new priestesses stood before the large gathering and were honored with songs, and finally glasses of wine were raised in the final acknowledgement of their achievement. The new priestesses sat down, and each High Priestess began giving promotions and new assignments to their temple priestesses. Again, they stood before us for songs and a glass of wine.

In each case my High Priestess was last to perform the initiations, promotions and new assignments. Having finished this, and after the priestesses sat back down, my High Priestess called for me to stand beside her.

"I have a special announcement." She said with a shaky voice.

The gathering got quiet and watched her intently.

"I have been the High Priestess here for a very long time." She said and smiled.

The gathering laughed at this, because she had remained the High Priestess for much longer than most.

"I have always asked the Gods for guidance, and I have always received answers to my questions." She said and looked from one side of the room to the other.

"Many years ago, I began asking if I should step down from being the High Priestess."

I looked at her and was sad to think she might no longer lead our temple.

"Yet," She continued, "I was always told the time had not come."

She looked at me, and back at the gathering.

"During this past new moon, I received a message. That message was that it is time to initiate a new High Priestess for this temple."

The gathering gasped, and I felt tears fill my eyes.

"I have loved my duties, I have loved the people I serve, and I am grateful for the blessings of the temple." She said and smiled. "I will continue doing my work, yet, I will not be the High Priestess."

I looked at the elder High Priestesses seated and saw most wiping tears from their eyes. Then I felt a hand on my shoulder and looked around to see the High Priestess looking at me.

"Give me your hand." She said.

I looked at the other priestess that had helped her this day while I was gone, she smiled with tears in her eyes, and I felt confused. The High Priestess took my hand and raised our arms up.

"The Gods spoke to me. They told me who would be the new High Priestess," she said loudly, "I stand with her now!"

I gasped while the people in the gathering room jumped to their feet, clapping and calling out thanks to the Mother. I looked at the High Priestess's face. There were many older and more experienced priestesses than me, that I expected would take her place.

"The Gods chose me?" I asked.

She nodded, dropped our arms down, and looked into my eyes.

"The Gods have spoken. You are to be the temple's new High Priestess."

"Did the Gods tell you why I was chosen?" I wanted to know.

She took in a big breath and let it out. Her eyes were sad.

"The Gods chose you because you are young and strong. In the future, you will still be young enough to face the changes that come."

I did not understand what she was saying.

She put her hand on my face, "I will be with you when that time comes."

CHAPTER 3

*T*he initiation for a new High Priestess, is witnessed by all the High Priestesses in a secret ceremony, done in a cave known only to them. This cave is mentioned in Atlantean mythology, and while many have looked for it, the location has remained a mystery.

"I will make arrangements with the others," The High Priestess said and pointed to the visiting High Priestesses, "we will do the initiation before they leave."

I nodded, still not believing this was real. "What do I do?"

"You need to fast and stay in the prayer hut by the river until we get you. We will lead you to the cave for your initiation."

"I need to tell my daughter that I will be gone." I said.

"I will send one of the new priestesses to stay with her." She told me, "Wear your temple jewelry to the hut, and we will bring you a new gown to wear."

THAT NIGHT I walked down the dirt trail through temple grounds to the river. It was a narrow trail, yet well used. Light from the big moon shone down between the trees, and I easily found where to place my feet. My heart pounded in my chest. I was excited yet afraid, I did not anticipate my fate was to be High Priestess, and I was unsure about my abilities to take on those responsibilities. My worry was interrupted by the sound of the river. I looked ahead and saw moon light shining down on the water, making it sparkle as it moved past.

"Have faith in yourself." I heard, and knew the Gods spoke to me.

I reached the river and stopped. I let my mind rest while admiring the water and decided to sit next to it. I closed my eyes and said devotions to the Mother, then opened my eyes and leaned forward to scoop water into my hand. The water was clear and cool, and I drank it.

"Thank you water," I said, "Thank you for your blessings."

I began to sing the temple song for honoring water, and enjoyed the sound of the river that seemed to sing with me. As I sat there, I felt my mind and body relax. I looked at the trail that continued next to the river, stood up and began to follow it.

❧

LAST NIGHT after walking further down the trail, I reached the prayer hut, fell on the bed and slept deeply all night. I awoke to sun light coming into the window and walked back outside. My stomach rumbled so I drank water from the river. I spent the day in prayer, picking flowers that grew wild near the hut, and enjoying the natural surroundings. After the sun had gone down behind the trees, I drank more water to fill my hungry stomach, and decided to lay down on the bed. I was not tired, yet I was so relaxed after spending my day here, that when I closed my eyes sleep came quickly.

❧

"WAKE."

I felt my shoulder shake, and I rolled over to see my High Priestess.

"It is time." She told me.

17

Behind her stood High Priestesses, and when I sat up, I saw more of them outside the small hut in the darkness.

"Stand." She said.

I stood and they took my gown off. I stood naked while a gown was passed from one High Priestess to the next, then it was slipped over my head and I looked down. The gown was heavy, yet very soft. Even in the dark of night I saw the deep color that shone with gold threads through it. The High Priestesses put my temple jewelry on me, and finally my High Priestess pulled a golden ring from her pocket. I recognized it. All the High Priestesses wore this ring.

"Give me your hand." She said.

I put my hand out to her, and noticed it was shaking.

"This ring carries the blessings of the Great Mother." She told me. "When you wear it, you represent the Great Mother in the temple."

She pushed the ring on my finger, it fit tight enough that it would not slip off. I held my hand up to see it, and other High Priestesses crowded in to see me wearing the new ring and new gown.

"We go now." My High Priestess said and led me outside.

We waited for the others to walk ahead of us on the trail by the river, then we followed. The moon was still big, and much light shone down on the trail and the river. We walked a long time, and I worried that my High Priestess and other elders would be tired, yet they seemed happy and sang songs.

The High Priestesses stopped, and we walked up behind them. I saw steps carved into stones that led up. There was a flat space at the top of the steps, and then I saw it. A rounded opening to a cave, with a golden glow that came from it. My heart began beating fast in my chest, and I watched as each High Priestess took the steps up, then disappeared into the cave. Finally, my High Priestess took my hand, and stepped ahead of me on the steps. I followed her up, making sure that she did not fall, and when we stood on the flat area at the top, she turned to face me.

"Do not be afraid." She said and led me into the cave.

We took a few steps before entering the cave, and I looked in to see the High Priestesses standing inside the cave. We walked through the center of them toward the back. The cave was lit, yet I did not see candles. As we walked, I began to feel strange. My body began to shake from the inside, then suddenly I felt as if I lifted up. I could not feel my feet walking on the floor of the cave, I turned to look at the High Priestess and was shocked. She was no longer the old woman with white hair! She was young again with long brown hair, she smiled and had a glow about her.

Then I felt something that made me look away from the High Priestess, and toward the back of the cave. I felt an overwhelming love. This feeling poured over me and into me, and my heart burst open. I looked ahead and saw golden light emanating from a very large person. As we got closer, I knew it was the Great Mother, even though the light obscured seeing her clearly.

My High Priestess bowed before her. "We bring you a new High Priestess."

I looked up to see a hand of golden light coming toward my forehead and saw no more.

~

I AWOKE TO FEELING COLD, hard stone beneath my body. I raised up to see early morning light streaming into the cave, and saw High Priestesses standing and sitting around me.

"Welcome back." My High Priestess said and held her hand out to me.

I stood up and looked around. "What happened? I do not understand."

"The Great Mother performed your initiation. We only assist." She told me.

"You looked young." I told her.

"Yes, when we entered the cave last night, we had to travel in spirit to the realm of the Great Mother." She said.

I looked around at the others who smiled back.

"You are now ready to learn knowledge that only High Priestesses may know."

I wondered what that knowledge might be.

"You will go to each temple for instruction by all of us."

We walked out of the cave and down the steps, I turned to look back and no longer saw the opening that we had entered last night. The stone steps went up to the flat area, and behind it was only the rock face of the mountain.

"Where did it go?" I asked.

My High Priestess smiled. "The Great Mother knows when to let us in."

～

WE WALKED ALONG THE RIVER, then up the trail to the temple, and entered the dining hall just as others were eating their morning meal.

"Welcome!" They called out to me.

I felt a new love for everyone here, as I walked to a table prepared for me. I saw my daughter jump up from her seat and run to me.

"Mother!" She cried out and put her arms around me, squeezing tightly.

I kissed her head and took her hand. She saw my new ring and held my hand up to see it closer.

"It is beautiful." She said and admired it.

In the daylight, I also saw it more clearly. The gold band had jewels of many colors embedded in it.

"Your gown is beautiful too!" My daughter said.

I lifted up the dark purple fabric and admired its softness. Golden thread was woven through it, and around the deep cut neckline and at the bottom of the sleeves, the gold thread looked solid from being sewn tightly together.

My stomached rumbled and I remembered that I had not eaten.

"Let us enjoy this delicious food!" I told her.

I let her sit next to me, as an attendant would, at the table of High Priestesses, and we had a joyous meal. We took extra time to eat, and many blessings were said for me and the temple.

CHAPTER 4

I looked around the room that has served me, and other High Priestesses before me. The windows went from my waist up above my head and ended in a half circle at the top, the floor was made of large squares of dark stone, the heavy wooden furniture was carved by artisans, and the cushions were filled with soft duck down. There were crystals on wooden stands, that stood by the windows and allowed the sun to shine on them. Birds carved from green stone sat on a branch that hung from the ceiling in the corner. In another corner, disguised as a carved wooden wall, was the entrance to the High Priestess alter room. This was a sacred room, and only High Priestesses were allowed in. The room was small and smelled of incense. There were objects left by the previous priestesses, and each time I entered, I felt their love and support. A small cushion lay on the floor before a low table and cabinet with incense and candles. I retreated there daily to connect with my Gods and to receive guidance. I also prayed for our people, the land and the animals. My responsibilities had grown with the size of our community, and many new challenges faced me that the former High Priestesses never dealt with.

~

WHILE BEING High Priestess was becoming more difficult, I found solace in watching my daughter grow. My father had found new teachers for her as she needed them, and her favorite was a teacher of science. She applied herself to her studies both in becoming a priestess at the temple, and in her scientific schooling. She never sought privilege because her mother was High Priestess, yet she took full advantage of my counsel when in the privacy of our home.

As she grew older, she asked her father for assistance to obtain an apprenticeship in a science lab. He was happy to help, and when he got her an apprenticeship under the tutelage of an advanced genetic scientist, she was ecstatic. She left early and often stayed late in the lab, she never considered it work because she enjoyed it so much.

I was well pleased with her accomplishments. I gave her the initiation, along with others, to be a new priestess in our temple, yet she took on minimal duties due to her work in the lab. Her genetics mentor advanced her to become his assistant, and he was proud of her innovations that assisted him greatly.

She grew tall with red hair like her father, had my delicate facial features, and was admired for her beauty and intelligence. Many men, some high-ranking officials and others of privileged families pursued her, yet she preferred to remain in the temple with me. She did not want to forsake her work in the lab, or her duties as a priestess, to become a mother and head of a household.

My daughter's childhood and adulthood to this point were wonderful experiences for both of us. We enjoyed our time together in the temple, and during the evening meal she regaled me with stories of her lab adventures. I believed that I would live out my life in the beauty of Atlantis, surrounded by family and friends. Yet, just as I did not foresee the future with my warrior and our daughter, I did not foresee the changes that would come.

~

As TIME PASSED, my daughter spent less time in the temple and more time in the lab. She stopped speaking about the work she was doing, only telling me that it was experimental. I began hearing disturbing stories from people that came to me for advice, stories about strange incidents at the lab. Incidents that made these people fearful to work there.

When I asked my daughter about the stories I was told, she hesitated before confessing that she and her mentor had been creating genetically altered beings. Beings that had gotten out of control and needed to be exterminated. My mouth fell open, I was astounded to learn this kind of work was being done.

"Why would you create these beings?" I asked.

She looked down, then back at me. I knew she felt guilty.

"We were asked to create new life, life that would serve us or work for us."

I was confused. "Slaves?"

"I did not think of creating slaves," she said, "yet they would be doing labor of different kinds."

I shook my head. "This is not what we believe in. You are a priestess and know this."

She nodded. "I have argued about doing this, yet I am only an assistant, and have no power to decide what kind of work we do."

I looked into her eyes. "It is time for you to leave that lab."

She nodded. "I have already asked to work in the energy lab and learn to work with the crystals."

I smiled, "Good!"

"I have been told the scientists are working with crystals to increase their power and output."

She was enthusiastic, and I thought my daughter had made a good choice, a safe choice.

∾

SHE GOT ACCEPTED to work with the crystals, and we resumed our pleasant life together. Her father visited and we had a long discussion about what had transpired in the genetics lab.

He shook his head, "I was told about those experiments, and they are evil."

"Evil?" I was shocked that he said that.

My daughter nodded. "Yes, they are evil mother. I did not tell you all we were doing."

I took in a deep breath and blew it out. "I am glad that you did not!"

"It is good that you left that lab!" Her father said and raised his glass of wine. "Well done!"

My daughter and I always enjoyed when her father visited. We loved him and we knew that he loved us. When he returned to Atlantis, he brought us gifts from his travels, and spent his precious free time with us. That night we shared many stories of what each of us had been doing, and after our daughter kissed us goodnight, we looked at each other knowing what would come next.

"I missed you." I told him.

"I always miss you when I am away." He said.

He stood up, walked to where I sat, and held out his hand.

"I want to lie with my woman." He said softly.

I took his hand and let him pull me up. I was his woman, the mother of his daughter, and we shared a love that had been foretold by my dear High Priestess that had passed many years before.

"Welcome home." I told him and led him toward my room.

∽

EACH TIME HE LEFT, I felt it was more difficult to be without him, and asked if he would someday remain in Atlantis to work.

"Yes." He told me and smiled, "I have requested this, but I have to wait for the order."

I shook my head. I knew his superiors considered him too valuable leading men outside of Atlantis, to bring him home soon.

"I look forward to that day." I said and reached out to touch his face. To me, he was still the most beautiful man that I had ever seen, and he had a great heart as well. I never tired of being with him, and I was sad when I had to watch him leave again.

CHAPTER 5

*M*y day was finally over. I had spent many hours teaching, counseling, and meeting with representatives of the community. I welcomed my walk home, through the gardens of the temple to my residence in the back of the grounds. The steps up to my house had large pots of flowers, and many places to sit on the expansive porch. I walked through the tall double doors and into a room with many windows and a high ceiling. I felt myself relax and headed to the kitchen to let the cook know I was home.

After changing into a simple dress of light cloth, I walked to the dining room and sat down at the table. I poured myself a glass of wine and wondered if I would see my daughter this evening. I was served my food and began eating when I heard my daughter's footsteps. I saw her walking toward me, and immediately noticed a concerned look on her face. She sat across from me and poured herself a glass of wine.

"What is worrying you?" I asked.

She shook her head, "We started something, and now we cannot stop it."

I didn't know what she meant, and I waited for her to explain.

"We learned how to increase the energy going into the crystals."

She told me, "but we didn't know how strong that energy would be, or how to redirect enough energy out of the crystals."

I shook my head, "I don't understand."

She looked into my eyes. "The crystals are receiving too much energy, and we don't know how to stop it or disperse enough of it from the crystals."

"What does that mean?" I asked.

"The crystals are getting overcharged," she said, "I'm afraid the biggest, the red crystal, will explode."

"Explode?" I repeated her word.

"If it blows up, all of Atlantis will be destroyed."

"What?" I could not believe what I was hearing.

"Scientists from other labs are helping," she told me, "we are working together to stop it."

"Good." I said, and silently prayed they would be successful.

$\sim$

THE FOLLOWING months were filled with meetings with scientists, warriors, High Priests and Priestesses, and ruling families from all over Atlantis. Fears were increasing. We feared that we would destroy ourselves, and we feared that invasive foreigners would take advantage of our problem, in an effort to destroy or subjugate us.

My daughter was in the lab from dawn until late at night, I rarely saw her and when I did, she looked aged from worry. She had not joined me for the evening meal since she told me about the crystal problem, so I was surprised to see her walk in and sit down at the table.

"I am happy to see you!" I said.

"I wanted to speak with you." She told me.

"Have you solved the problem?" I asked.

She looked at me, her lips were tight, her eyes were sad, and she shook her head.

"We have not been able to stop the energy going into the crystal, and we have not learned how to redirect enough energy out of the crystal to discharge it."

"What does this mean?" I asked.

"The crystal is dangerously over-charged," she said, "I'm afraid it's ready to explode."

"Oh no!" I cried out. "What will we do?"

"You need to leave." My daughter said.

My mouth fell open, I heard her say "You must leave," yet I assumed she meant we would leave together.

"Mother." She said gently, "You are a High Priestess, you need to lead people to safety."

I knew this was a duty I was expected to perform, yet I hoped it would not be needed.

"Have you sent messengers to the other temples?" I asked.

"Yes." She said.

"When the time comes," I told her, "We will leave and take the priestesses and families that serve us."

"You must start preparing to leave now." She told me.

"Now?" I asked.

She nodded her head. "Yes."

"When will we leave?" I asked.

She took in a breath and blew it out with a sigh.

"I cannot leave, I am responsible for working with the crystal."

"You are also a priestess!" I told her, "You are needed by the people."

"I can help most by staying and trying to stop what we've started." She insisted.

I felt tears well up in my eyes. "I cannot leave you."

She also had tears in her eyes. "You have no other choice."

My heart sank. I could not imagine life without her, then suddenly a picture came into my mind. I saw myself leaving Atlantis without her, I gasped and began shaking.

"No!" I cried out with the deepest pain that I had ever felt. "No!"

She walked around the table to hold me and whispered. "Not everyone can leave."

I felt sick when she said this. "Have you told your grandfather?"

She nodded. "He is preparing to send the family and servants first, he said he cannot leave yet."

I knew my father had many business ventures that he would not abandon.

"He said he would have a boat for himself ready to leave." She told me.

I shook my head, knowing my father was taking a chance with his life. I thought of the people in Atlantis, people that did not have boats to leave and was overwhelmed with grief for them.

"What of the people?" I asked.

She looked at me with great sadness. "If the crystal explodes, it will happen so quickly they will not suffer."

"I pray this is so." I told her.

～

I AWOKE EARLY the next morning, and my daughter had already left for the lab. I sipped my tea, looked out at the garden, and thought about what she told me. It was impossible to accept that I must leave, and worst of all, to leave my daughter. I wanted to talk to her father, to ask him what he thought. He often had information that my daughter wasn't aware of.

"I wonder where he is?" I thought.

I didn't have to wonder long. I left my house and as I walked through the garden, I saw him walking toward me, wearing the protective clothing he traveled in. I was relieved and happy to see him.

"I wanted to see you." I told him.

He smiled, "I am glad to see you."

We found a bench in the shade, I sat beside him and looked into his face. He had grown older, now having lines around his eyes and mouth, and the curls of red hair shone with strands of silver.

"Our daughter tells me that I must prepare to leave Atlantis." I said and watched his expression.

He nodded. "That would be best."

I shook my head, "How can I leave? Where will I go?"

He took my hand in his and squeezed it.

"I will get a good boat, and I will command trusted men to protect you."

I looked into his eyes. "Where will you be?"

"I will be here watching over our daughter." He said.

I shook my head. "No, no!"

"I have my orders to stay in Atlantis." He told me.

"And I must leave!" I cried out.

How could this be? Was this really happening? I collapsed against his chest, sobbing.

He put his arms around me, and for a moment I felt safe. Then the horror flooded back in.

"I can't leave you!" I cried and leaned against him.

"I will come get you after the danger passes." He told me.

I looked up with hope, yet when I saw his eyes, I knew he did not believe his words.

I reached up and encircled his neck with my arms. "I love you."

"I love you." He said.

I leaned forward and kissed him. He held me tightly, and we kissed long and tenderly. I did not want to believe that I would lose both him and our daughter.

Afterwards, we sat silently looking at each other. I did not see the flowers nor smell their fragrance, they disappeared as I looked into his eyes. I wanted only to see his face.

"I will remember your face." I thought, "I will remember your beautiful face."

Then he stood up and pulled me up to face him.

"I will send a warrior when the boat is ready." He told me.

"Thank you." I said, "I will tell my people to prepare."

He wrapped his arms around me, then kissed me on top of my head and let go.

"I need to leave." He said.

"Will I see you before I go." I told him.

He nodded, "I will see you."

Then he turned and walked away. I watched him walk through the garden, until he left the temple gate and I could see him no more.

～

MY HEART WAS BROKEN, my world had collapsed, I grieved losing my daughter and her father already. I did not want to give up hope, yet my inner knowing had already faced the truth. I would leave and they would no longer be in my life. I would face my future in a strange place, where I would have to be strong for those that depended on me, yet I would have no one to lean on for comfort.

I heard a bird singing near me and turned to see it sitting on a branch. It stopped singing and didn't move, it was watching me. Then suddenly I realized that the bird's singing reminded me of a song my High Priestess used to sing. Tears streamed down my face, I remembered what she told me and her promise to me. I nodded and understood. These were the changes she told me of, this was how the temple would be saved, and, this was why the Gods chose me.

CHAPTER 6

Another month passed and the priestesses, my servants, and the families that served the temple were ready to leave. I had packed sacred items for a new temple into a heavy wooden trunk, which sat in a hall of the temple, and I kept a trunk packed with personal items near my bed. I was ready to go, yet prayed each day, that I would not have to leave.

I saw my daughter only in passing, she spent all her waking hours at the lab. Her father joined me when he could, often late in the evening. I bathed him, rubbed oil into his sore muscles, and savored our love late into the night. It was after such a night, that we lay together in bed. He turned on his side to face me, stroked my hair, and I saw tears in his eyes.

"What is wrong?" I asked.

"The boat is ready," he said, "my men have their orders."

I shook my head. "No, no, I cannot leave yet."

He took my face in his hands. "It is time."

We did not sleep that night. We talked, kissed and held each other until the sun rose. I watched him dress and walked with him from my room.

"Will you eat?" I asked.

He shook his head, and I saw the strain of his feelings upon his face.

"I will see you again." He told me.

My eyes were filled with tears, and I wanted to believe him. I nodded.

"I will see you again." I said.

He turned, walked down the steps, through the garden and out of my life.

~

I FELT SO wretched that I could not eat, and my hands shook so much that I could barely dress. I left my house, and arrived at the temple not knowing how I got there. I couldn't speak as I passed priestesses, and after closing the door behind me, I collapsed onto a chair. The room spun, and I tried to grab a table, then darkness fell over me.

"Priestess! Priestess!" I heard and felt someone shaking my shoulder.

Someone lifted me off the floor and put me back on my chair.

"What happened?" I asked.

"You fell from your chair. Are you hurt?"

I sat for a moment, trying to remember what had happened. "No, I am not hurt."

"Drink this." A priestess told me, and lifted a cup of tea to my lips.

I sipped the tea, and my mind slowly awoke to the nightmare that was now my life.

"It is time." I told her.

"Time?" She asked.

"It is time to leave." I said.

I saw the fear in her eyes and understood, yet I had to be strong.

"Tell the others we will be leaving this day."

She nodded, placed the tea on the table beside my chair, and left the room. She did not close the door, and another priestess came in to stay with me.

"Send a message to my daughter." I told her, "Tell her to meet me in the inner temple when the sun is directly overhead."

The priestess left me, and I sat looking around. I saw the crystals with sunlight shining through them, the green birds that swung on the branch when wind blew in, and then I saw the door to my private alter. I put my hands on the chair and pushed up. My legs still felt weak, yet I walked to the door. I pushed on the carved wood, it swung inward, and I stepped through.

"What will I take?" I thought and looked around at all the items left behind from other High Priestesses.

I grabbed as many as I could, using my gown to hold them in front of me.

"Please travel with me." I asked the Great Mother, yet I knew she would.

∾

THE WARRIORS COMMANDED to protect me arrived at the temple, they were to escort us to the boat. There were many trunks of personal belongings, food, and things needed for a new temple, piled on wagons and carts ready to go. The warriors, priestesses, families and servants, stood waiting for me in the courtyard. I walked out to the covered porch and took a deep breath. I must forget my fear and my sadness, I must guide them as the Great Mother now.

"Take them to the boat," I told the warriors in a strong voice, "after you have loaded the boat, come back for me."

I watched them leave and looked up at the sun, it was high overhead, so I walked into the temple. The inner temple was a sacred place. A place that only priestesses were allowed, a place that was used for sacred ceremonies and advanced spiritual work. I walked past the large gathering room to a long hallway that went deep into the temple. As I approached the inner temple, white pillars began to appear on each side of the walkway. I looked ahead and saw solid marble walls facing me, with a tall golden door that was partially open. My heart began to pound.

"Can I do this?" I thought.

∾

I WALKED through the doors and saw only white. The floor, the high ceiling, the walls and more pillars. I walked further into the room until I stood next to a pillar, looking into the inner temple where so many times in the past, I had felt the Great Mother's presence.

Although the Great Mother had shown me visions of this day, I knew where we would land, and how we would travel to a new place to rebuild our lives. I had not been shown that I must leave the two I loved most.

Then I saw my daughter across the room and caught my breath. I stood watching my beloved pace. She walked back and forth at the rear of the inner temple and the silhouette of her long, black gown contrasted sharply with the white marble. I admired her red hair which fell down her back, and I memorized every exquisite detail of her.

I waited not wanting to ask, yet compelled as a mother, needing to know there was nothing more I could do. She had told me her decision. I knew that I could not persuade her, nor alter her course. My chest was tight, so tight it was hard to breath. Tears spilled down my face.

"Are you sure?" I asked and my words echoed across the room.

She stopped and turned to look at me with great pain in her eyes. I wanted to comfort her, to console her as I had when she was young.

"You must go." She said firmly, "You must go now."

How could I leave her? My child, my heart. I wanted to hold her just once more, to try and change her mind, yet I sank into the knowing that we would never see each other again. I nodded. My throat had tightened so much, that I had to will my body to speak those final words.

"I love you."

"I love you." She said, then turned away and began her pacing again.

I knew her scientific mind was working, thinking of what else she might do to prevent the inevitable, so I looked once more at my beloved before spinning on my heel to leave.

～

THAT WAS my final day as a High Priestess on Atlantis. The warriors came for me, and soon I stood in the middle of a large, sturdy wooden boat. I looked over the people sitting around me, then put my hand above my eyes to shield the bright sunlight, and looked across the blue water of the sea. Far away on the horizon, I saw the high barren cliffs that had come to me in dreams.

"There." I called out for all to hear.

I pointed my arm toward the horizon and called out again. "We go there."

I felt the boat jerk and move beneath me, as the men pulled back on the long oars. I heard people speaking around me, and felt their excitement and fear, yet my mind traveled beyond the boat.

I had left my daughter and my warrior behind. I had left my home, temple and way of life. I knew not where my family was, or if my father would leave for safety. My life as I knew it was over, and I felt overwhelmed with personal loss and grief. Tears rolled down my face, and I quickly wiped them away.

I heard a voice in my head, and knew it was the High Priestess that had chosen me for this time. "I am with you." She whispered.

I nodded, I knew this to be true. I took in a breath and told my heart it need not pound so hard. I felt the tears in my eyes wanting to pour out, yet I told them we would cry later. I realized my hands were clinched into fists, and I brought them up to a prayer position, praying silently for the strength and the resolve I needed.

I gazed at those in the boat, and suddenly felt love and compassion flood my heart. I realized these people, and others, would be my new family. I would assist, guide and love them as I stepped upon a path devoted to the greater good of all. I now understood, with all I am, and will be.

"I walk as the Great Mother."

ABOUT THE AUTHOR

APRIL AUTRY

April writes about her spiritual journey, including many of her past lives.

April is an intuitive mentor, Quantum healer, Reiki master, yoga teacher, and teaches alignment of your mind-body-soul through consciousness expansion and spiritual practices.

Books, meditations, courses and spiritual lifestyle products can be found on her website:

GalacticGrandmother.com

April enjoys reading your book reviews, so please feel free to email her at:

info@galacticgrandmother.com